Mohandas GANDHI

DAVID DOWNING

www.heinemann.co.uk/library
Visit our website to find out more information about Heinemann Library books.

To order:
☎ Phone 44 (0) 1865 888066
🗎 Send a fax to 44 (0) 1865 314091
💻 Visit the Heinemann Bookshop at www.heinemann.co.uk/library to browse our catalogue and order online.

First published in Great Britain by Heinemann Library,
Halley Court, Jordan Hill, Oxford OX2 8EJ,
a division of Reed Educational and Professional Publishing Ltd.
Heinemann is a registered trademark of Reed Educational and Professional Publishing Ltd.

OXFORD MELBOURNE AUCKLAND
JOHANNESBURG BLANTYRE GABORONE
IBADAN PORTSMOUTH (NH) USA CHICAGO

Designed by AMR
Illustrated by Art Construction
Originated by Dot Gradations
Printed in China

ISBN 0 431 13868 0
06 05 04 03 02
10 9 8 7 6 5 4 3 2 1

British Library Cataloguing in Publication Data
Downing, David
 Mohandas Gandhi. – (Leading lives)
 1.Gandhi, M. K. (Mohandas Karamchand), 1869–1948
 2.Statesmen – India – Biography – Juvenile literature
 3.India – Politics and government – 1765–1947 – Juvenile
 literature 4.India – History – British occupation, 1765–1947 – Juvenile literature
 I.Title
 954'.035'092

Acknowledgements
The publishers would like to thank the following for permission to reproduce photographs:
Ann and Bury Peerless: pp. 6, 52; Camera Press: pp. 8, 37, 55; Hulton Archive: pp. 17, 18, 26, 29, 30, 33, 35, 43, 50; Mary Evans: p. 36; Popperfoto: pp. 4, 44, 47, 51; Stone: p. 11; Topham: pp. 7, 13, 20, 22, 25, 28, 34, 41, 49.

Cover photograph reproduced with permission of Hulton Getty.

Every effort has been made to contact copyright holders of any material reproduced in this book. Any omissions will be rectified in subsequent printings if notice is given to the publishers.

Our thanks to Christopher Gibb and Philip Emmett for their comments in the preparation of this book.

Disclaimer
All the Internet addresses (URLs) given in this book were valid at the time of going to press. However, due to the dynamic nature of the Internet, some addresses may have changed, or sites may have ceased to exist since publication. While the author and publishers regret any inconvenience this may cause readers, no responsibility for any such changes can be accepted by either the author or the publishers.

Any words appearing in the text in bold, **like this**, are explained in the Glossary.

Contents

1 A piece of salt

It is early April 1930. In the Indian province of Gujarat, a huge column of men and women is slowly winding its way south towards the sea.

This is no ordinary procession. For one thing, it is being watched by journalists from all around the world; for another, it contains an amazing mixture of people, from poor **peasants** in **loincloths** to the most important leaders of India's **nationalist** movement in their smart caps and tailored tunics. They are walking a road watered against the dust and carpeted with flower petals for the bare feet of the marchers. They are walking behind a scrawny, half-naked, 60-year-old man by the name of Mohandas Gandhi.

▲ Gandhi, centre left with bare chest, sets off from Sabarmati on his 160-kilometre (100-mile) march to the sea.

Gandhi had once studied law in London, and had been a lawyer in South Africa. He is now the British **Empire's** most dangerous opponent. Others around the world have attacked British rule, but none have hit the British so hard where it really hurts – in their image of themselves, in their consciences. Many have argued against the Empire, but few have shown it so clearly and simply for what it is – an instrument for the exploitation of one people by another.

This march to the sea is a case in point. Gandhi is not leading protesters to hurl violent slogans, storm police stations or fight street battles. He is going to the beach to pick up a piece of salt. A peaceful act that can hurt no one, but which happens to be illegal – only India's foreign rulers have the right to India's salt.

The world will watch as he breaks the law and demonstrates the injustice of Empire. In a few weeks he will be arrested, but by then thousands of others will be following his example. They too will be arrested, until the prisons are bursting and the British have made themselves look petty, foolish and vindictive.

The truth of India's situation will be there for all to see, and Indians, by sticking with non-violence, will not have lowered themselves to the level of their opponents. On the contrary, Indian self-respect will rise as British self-respect declines, bringing both rulers and ruled to a new understanding of their basic equality as human beings. This will trigger the end of Empire and the birth of an India worthy of independence. And all from a piece of salt.

Childhood and youth

Mohandas Karamchand Gandhi was born in Porbandar, a white-walled Indian city overlooking the Arabian Sea, on 2 October 1869. Porbandar was a tiny, semi-independent state, one of hundreds in British India, and Mohandas's father Karamchand Gandhi was its *diwan*, or prime minister.

▼ *The view from the Gandhi family home in Porbandar.*

Karamchand Gandhi was considered fair-minded, incorruptible and truthful, and Mohandas certainly inherited these qualities from his father. His mother, Putlibai, probably influenced him even more. She was very religious, but in an unusually broad-minded way. The Gandhis were **Hindus**, but Putlibai was quite willing to accept that India's other major religion, **Islam**, offered an equally valid path to God. Both religions distinguished between right and wrong, both encouraged people to pray, meditate and behave better. Putlibai visited the **temple** every day, and often **fasted** for religious reasons. To the young Mohandas she seemed a saintly figure, and a wonderful example of a life given over to serving others.

The family shared a large, three-storey house with the families of Karamchand's five brothers, so Mohandas never suffered from a shortage of uncles, aunts and cousins. He had two half-sisters from his father's earlier marriages, one elder sister, Ralitabehn, and two elder brothers, Lakshmidas and Karsandas.

Hinduism and caste

Some 70% of the population of British India were, like Gandhi and his family, Hindus. Hinduism is one of the world's oldest religions, stretching back over five millennia. It recognizes one great power (Brahman), which is present in everything. A large number of gods and goddesses reflect different facets of that power. There are many holy books, but no single teacher or prophet. Hindus believe in reincarnation, the transfer of the soul after death to another person, animal or plant. The aim of every Hindu is to break free from this circle of endless rebirth and become part of Brahman.

Hindu society was divided into four hierarchical **castes**, and these into hundreds of sub-castes. Those who did the lowest, dirtiest jobs were outside the four castes, and were called **Untouchables**.

The young boy

Mohandas was a shy, nervous boy. He was afraid of the dark, of snakes and thieves and ghosts. He had large ears, large eyes and an infectious smile, and from an early age he showed himself sensitive to the sufferings of others. On one occasion he climbed a mango tree to bandage the damaged, 'wounded' fruit. His schoolwork was erratic. One report thought him 'good at English, fair in arithmetic and weak in geography'. His conduct was good, his handwriting bad. He played cricket and tennis, but did not really like sports.

▶ *A photograph of the 7-year-old Mohandas Gandhi.*

▲ *Gandhi as a teenager (right) with his older brother Lakshmidas.*

He was very honest. When a group of youngsters were taken to task for the attempted theft of some bronze statues from the local temple, the 6-year-old Mohandas was the only one to own up. On another occasion, a teacher who wanted to impress a visiting school inspector encouraged him to cheat in a spelling test, but the young Gandhi chose to ignore the hint.

Marriage and rebellion

Marriage at a young age was usual in India at this time, and at 13 years old Mohandas was married to Kasturbai, a girl of the same age whom his parents had chosen for him. In later life Gandhi would campaign against child marriage, remembering how difficult he had found the first few years of his own.

He was obsessed with Kasturbai, but guilty about this feeling. He tried to make her into an obedient wife, to restrict her freedom, but she refused to follow his orders, and went out on her own whenever she felt like it. He was forced to recognize that she had rights, too.

Mohandas was also learning a lot from a **Muslim** friend, Sheik Mehtab, who encouraged him to rebel against the restrictions of Hindu life, and particularly the belief that eating meat was wrong. Mehtab persuaded Mohandas that the British rulers of India were strong because they ate meat, and could only be opposed by other meat-eaters. In secret, the two friends cooked and ate a tough piece of goat's meat, but Mohandas was promptly sick. That night he felt so guilty for eating the meat that he dreamed there was a live goat bleating in his stomach.

The two friends also stole coins from servants to buy cigarettes, but the young Gandhi's days as a thief were few because of his unfailing honesty. On another occasion, after stealing part of a gold **amulet** from his brother to pay off the same brother's debts, he felt compelled to write a letter of confession to his father. Karamchand wept and embraced his son.

Deciding his future

Around this time his father became seriously ill with an ulcer. Mohandas helped to nurse him, sitting with him and giving him a leg massage every evening. But on the day his father died, Mohandas was with Kasturbai. The young Gandhi never forgave himself. Kasturbai, then aged 15, was already pregnant, and when the baby died at birth, Mohandas thought God was punishing him for his selfishness.

It had long been expected that Mohandas would follow in his father's footsteps. After finishing school aged 17, he attended a Gujarati college for a term, but enjoyed neither the place nor his studies. The family considered sending him to England, where he could take a law degree, and despite the birth of his first son Harilal in the early summer of 1888, he decided that this was his best option. After promising his mother not to touch meat or alcohol or women, Gandhi sailed for England, leaving Kasturbai and his infant son behind.

British India

In the late 19th century, British India was made up of present-day India, Pakistan, Bangladesh and Burma. In religious terms, the population (292 million in 1900) was roughly 70% Hindu, 25% Muslim, 2% Christian, 2% Sikh and 1% Buddhist or Jain. Over 30 major languages were spoken. The British directly ruled some of the numerous states, while others, particularly the smaller ones, were allowed to keep the appearance of a fictional independence under their traditional rulers. A few Indians were very rich, but most were involved in a constant struggle to survive off the land.

3 England and the law

On the long voyage to England, Gandhi had a foretaste of problems to come. The meals aboard ship were a nightmare. He had no skill with a knife and fork – many Indians eat with their fingers – and the menu contained nothing for **vegetarians**. After a few days, he gave up eating in the ship's restaurant, preferring to live off the limited supply of fruit and sweets he had brought in his trunk. When the ship finally docked at Southampton he stepped ashore in a thin, white, cotton suit, only to find that everyone else was dressed in dark, heavy clothes.

Homesick, lonely and lacking in confidence, it took him a while to settle down. His English was not very good, and his landlady had never heard of vegetarianism. She did her best, though, feeding him porridge for breakfast, and spinach, bread and jam for both lunch and dinner.

Fitting in

Gandhi enrolled for his law studies and began taking English lessons. He decided that dressing and behaving like an Englishman would help him to fit in. He bought a complete new outfit from the Army & Navy Stores and an extremely expensive evening dress suit. He bought himself dancing lessons, only to discover that he had no sense of rhythm. **Elocution** and violin lessons followed, but proved just as unsuccessful.

▶ *Gandhi, smartly dressed in the English style, as a law student in London.*

Fashion victim

'He was wearing at the time a high silk top hat "burnished bright", a stiff and starched collar, a rather flashy tie displaying all the colours of the rainbow, under which there was a fine striped silk shirt. He wore as his outer clothes a morning coat, a double-breasted waistcoat, and dark striped trousers to match, and not only patent-leather shoes but spats over them. He also carried leather gloves and a silver-mounted stick, but wore no spectacles. His clothes were regarded as the very acme of fashion for young men about town ...'

(Gandhi, as described by Sachchidananda Sinha, another Indian student in London)

Then Gandhi had a stroke of luck, chancing upon a vegetarian restaurant in London's Farringdon Street. He filled his stomach for the first time since his arrival in England, and purchased a book at the restaurant, Henry Salt's *A Plea for Vegetarianism*. Reading the book helped convince him not to eat meat on principle.

He soon became friendly with other regular diners, most of whom were members of the Vegetarian Society of England. He joined the society and over the next two years wrote several articles for its journal. He had found somewhere to fit in.

As a boy Gandhi had not been particularly religious, but many of his Vegetarian Society friends were interested in Indian religions.

▲ *Gandhi (sitting front left) and members of the Vegetarian Society.*

They introduced him to the epic religious poem, the
Bhagavad Gita, which he would find such an inspiration in
later life. He also read the Christian New Testament and was
deeply moved by Jesus's Sermon on the Mount, with its
insistence on non-violence.

The shy lawyer
The three years went slowly by. Gandhi studied hard and
explored the streets of London on long walks. He was careful
with money, but managed to visit Paris in 1890 to see the
famous Exhibition and new Eiffel Tower.

He cooked for friends, and occasionally played bridge, but his shyness persisted: 'the presence of half a dozen or more people would strike me dumb'.

Gandhi passed his examinations, was **called to the Bar** on 10 June 1891, and set sail for home two days later. He arrived back in India to find his mother had died several months earlier. Events over the next few months did little to raise his spirits. Neither his wife nor brothers were interested in knives and forks, porridge or European clothes, and his career as a lawyer got off to a bad start. One case in Bombay ended in disaster when he felt too shy to speak up on behalf of his client.

In Porbandar, his brother Lakshmidas had been dismissed from his job as the local ruler's secretary after falling out with a British agent. Gandhi had briefly met this Englishman in London, and Lakshmidas hoped his younger brother could persuade the agent to reverse the decision. Gandhi disapproved of such unofficial approaches, but reluctantly agreed to try. The agent disapproved of them, too, and after an angry discussion Gandhi was rudely shown the door.

He later claimed this incident 'changed the entire course of my life', and it certainly made him disillusioned with the small state politics which had been his father's life. When he received an offer from the **Muslim** Indian firm of Dada Abdullah to represent them in a South African legal dispute, he was only too happy to accept. Expecting to be away for less than a year, he left Kasturbai behind once more, along with sons Harilal and the recently born Manilal.

4 Birth of a rebel

Soon after arriving in South Africa, Gandhi arranged a business meeting in the Transvaal capital Pretoria. He bought a first-class ticket for the journey from Durban, but when the train reached Maritzburg a white passenger took one look at Gandhi in his first-class compartment and angrily went to fetch two officials. They told him that only white people were permitted to travel first class. When he refused to travel in the third-class carriage they made him get off the train, and he spent the whole night on the freezing Maritzburg platform, brooding on the injustice he had suffered.

Should he give up and go home to India? Should he forget about the train incident and carry on with the legal case? Or should he stay and fight for justice, for himself and his fellow-Indians? He decided in favour of the latter. It was, he later said, one of the defining moments of his life.

His northward journey continued to be eventful. One section was by stagecoach, and the conductor insisted that Gandhi sit next to the driver rather than ride in comfort inside. Later, when the conductor wanted to sit outside and smoke, he demanded that Gandhi perch on the footboard. When Gandhi refused, he dragged him off the coach and beat him until the other passengers intervened.

In Johannesburg, Gandhi was not allowed into the Grand National Hotel, but on the train to Pretoria an Englishman stood up for him when another conductor tried to have him ejected from the first-class compartment. This, and similar support from white guests at his Pretoria hotel, encouraged him. Many whites obviously knew, deep in their hearts, that racial discrimination was wrong. He could appeal to their better nature.

Gandhi's South Africa

In May 1893, when Gandhi's boat arrived in Durban, the area now known as South Africa was still a patchwork of British colonies (Cape Colony and Natal), independent **Boer** republics (Transvaal and the Orange Free State) and loosely-defined tribal areas. The population of the whole area comprised around two million black people, half a million whites and some 80,000 Indians. About half the Indians were indentured labourers, people who had come from India to work on white-owned farms for a five-year period. They were paid next to nothing, and had virtually no rights. The other half, the 'free Indians', were tradesmen, artisans, and professionals like Gandhi.

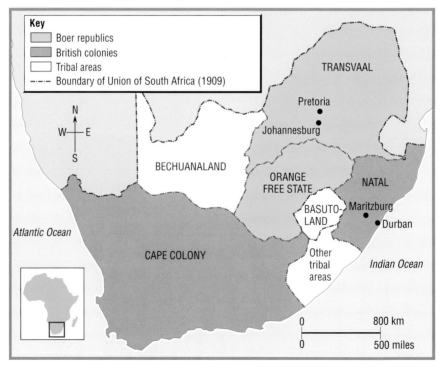

▲ *Southern Africa in Gandhi's time.*

No ordinary rebel

A few days after his arrival in Pretoria he called a meeting of all the Indians in the city and discovered, much to his own amazement, that the events of the past week had cured him of his shyness as a public speaker. He told the meeting about his own experiences of racial discrimination and listened to those of other Indians: they could not own land or vote, they could neither be out after 9 p.m. nor use the pavements during the day.

What could they do about all this? An ordinary rebel would have simply protested against the behaviour of those in authority, but Gandhi was never an ordinary rebel. He told the other Indians that they must first show themselves worthy of equality. They must learn to speak English, clean up their neighbourhoods, and always be completely straight in their business dealings. **Hindus** and **Muslims** must respect and get on with each other. Then they could demand equality with a good conscience.

Gandhi got on with the case he had been hired to handle. He quickly realized that only greedy lawyers benefited from long court cases. A good lawyer's job was to gather evidence, get to the truth of the matter quickly, and then negotiate a solution that was in the best interests of both parties. Soon he had achieved this for his client, and looked forward to returning to India.

▶ *Gandhi sitting outside his Johannesburg law office in 1905. Henry Polak (seated left) and Gandhi's secretary, Sonya Schlesin (right), were two of his earliest white supporters.*

YOU CAN LOCATE THE PLACES WHERE GANDHI WENT IN SOUTH AFRICA ON THE MAP ON PAGE 16.

Making himself unpopular

But then, at a farewell party in Durban, Gandhi discovered that the Government of Natal was about to take voting rights away from those few Indians who had them. This must be resisted, he told his friends. They begged him to stay and lead the resistance. He agreed to postpone his departure for a month.

He organized a 10,000-signature **petition** and set up the **Natal Indian Congress** to campaign for Indian rights. Once again he stressed this was not just a political struggle, not just about changing government policies; it was also a social and educational struggle, about changing people.

A matter of rights

'I discovered that as a man and as an Indian I had no rights. More correctly, I discovered that I had no rights as a man because I was an Indian.'

(Gandhi, speaking in South Africa)

The month became a year and Gandhi, realizing that he would probably be in South Africa for many more, went home to India to collect Kasturbai and his two sons. Their ship, which was also carrying hundreds of Indian immigrants, reached Durban late in December 1896, but it was mid-January before they were allowed to dock. The white officials were reluctant to allow so many new immigrants ashore, and they were particularly angry with Gandhi, whose speeches in India criticizing the South African authorities had been reported in the press. Eventually Kasturbai and the children were successfully smuggled ashore, but Gandhi himself was caught by a white mob, kicked and punched. He might have been severely injured but for the timely intervention of the local police chief's wife. She got him to the house of an Indian merchant, and when this was surrounded by the mob, he escaped out the back.

It was a shocking introduction to South Africa for Kasturbai, and there were more shocks in store. Over the last few years her husband had been simplifying his lifestyle. His law practice had made him rich, but he insisted on cutting his own hair and doing his own laundry, so that he could spend more on helping the poor. His house was full of strangers, some of whom turned out to be **Untouchables**, to Kasturbai's horror. They argued long and hard about this, and it would be some years before she came to accept his unconventional practices. Over the next three years she gave birth to another two sons, Ramdas in 1897 and Devadas in 1900.

War

In 1899, the second **Boer War** broke out between Britain and the two Boer republics of Transvaal and the Orange Free State. Gandhi supported the British, arguing that because he was demanding rights from the **Empire** he owed it a debt of duty. His offer to form an Indian ambulance unit was eventually accepted, and he and many others received medals for their brave service. Their loyal involvement in the war changed the way South Africa's Indians were seen by the British, and in 1901, Gandhi felt able to take his family back to India.

▶ *British soldiers crossing a river during the Boer War.*

Ambulance man

'After a night's work, which had shattered men with much bigger frames, I came across Gandhi in the early morning sitting by the roadside eating a regulation army biscuit. Every man in Buller's force was dull and depressed, and damnation was invoked on everything. But Gandhi was stoical in his bearing, cheerful and confident in his conversations, and had a kindly eye. He did one good.'

(British journalist Vere Stent, writing about his meeting with Gandhi during the Boer War Battle of Spion Kop)

▲ Gandhi's Indian Ambulance Corps during the Boer War.

5 *Satyagrahi*

Back in India, Gandhi attended an **Indian National Congress** meeting in Calcutta. He was looking forward to renewing **nationalist** contacts made during his visit in 1896, but many participants seemed more concerned with upholding **caste** status, arguing that only **Untouchables** should clean the toilets. Gandhi set an example of equality amongst **Hindus** by picking up a mop and bucket.

He set up a new law practice in Bombay, but the business was only a few months old when he received an urgent summons from the Indian community in South Africa. The gains made during the **Boer War** had evaporated, and he was needed once more.

A simpler life

Indians were now treated worse in Transvaal than Natal, so Gandhi decided to establish the family home and law practice in Johannesburg. He started a newspaper, *Indian Opinion*, early in 1903 to cover the affairs of the Indian community. This was printed over 640 kilometres (400 miles) away in Durban, and Gandhi often had to make the day-long journey by train. On one such trip, he read a book that profoundly influenced him for the rest of his life: *Unto This Last* by John Ruskin. The author argued that the more an individual gave to society, the more he or she gained. He stressed that all individuals were equally valuable members of the human race, that, for example, barbers were just as important as lawyers. He also believed a life of manual labour was the most fulfilling life.

YOU CAN LOCATE THE PLACES WHERE GANDHI WENT IN SOUTH AFRICA ON THE MAP ON PAGE 16.

Ruskin's arguments fitted in with his own beliefs, and encouraged Gandhi to change his life. The *Indian Opinion* printshop was moved to a 40-hectare plot of land 22 kilometres (14 miles) outside Durban, and homes were built for the workers and their families.

Phoenix Farm, as the new settlement was called, would be a self-sufficient **commune**, where everyone would grow their own food and earn the same wages.

For the next few years, Gandhi divided his time between the farm and his law practice in Johannesburg. During this period he read and talked a lot about religion. He befriended a group of **Quakers**, and studied both the Christian Bible and the **Muslim Koran**. The main problem with Christianity, he thought, was its failure to love and respect all living things. The main problem with **Hinduism** was the caste system, and particularly the appalling treatment of the Untouchables.

He continued to simplify and purify his life. According to the ***Bhagavad Gita***, material possessions made it harder to reap **spiritual** rewards, so Gandhi gave most of his away. Sexual desire made it difficult for him to focus on what he felt was truly important in life, and in 1906, aged 37, he took a **vow** of **celibacy**.

▲ *Members of Phoenix Farm, the commune in South Africa where Gandhi and other Indian families lived and worked, in 1906.*

Satyagraha

Later that same year the Transvaal authorities, now under **Boer** control, introduced a new law requiring Indians – and only Indians – to register, have their fingerprints taken, and carry passes at all times. This was a clear case of **racial discrimination**, and Gandhi called a protest meeting in a Johannesburg theatre. Thousands of Indians attended. When one man passionately promised to take a vow of resistance, Gandhi pointed out how important it was to take such vows seriously. The consequences of such disobedience, he pointed out, would probably include threats, beatings and prison. The audience did not care. They all swore to resist the new law.

A mystery

'It has always been a mystery to me how men can feel themselves honoured by the humiliation of their fellow beings.'

(Gandhi, speaking in South Africa)

Gandhi's strategy for the campaign was simple. They would ignore the new rules and, if threatened with violence, refuse to fight back. The protesters did not need the force of violence because they already had **satyagraha** – the 'force of truth' – on their side. The **satyagrahis**, as he called the non-violent protesters, should never forget that it was evils they were fighting, not individuals. They should always treat the latter with courtesy. Indeed, in the years to come, Gandhi would nearly always send his opponents a polite warning when action was imminent.

The campaign went well. Only a few hundred of the 13,000 Indians in Transvaal registered, and the authorities responded by arresting Gandhi and other prominent leaders.

This achieved nothing, so General Jan Smuts, the minister in charge of Indian affairs, offered to release the prisoners and abandon the new law if the Indians would only agree to register voluntarily. Gandhi accepted the deal: a *satyagrahi* had to trust his opponent, whether or not the opponent deserved such trust.

Smuts did not. The law was not repealed, and Gandhi led 2000 protesters in burning their certificates of registration. He and many others, including his son Harilal, were re-arrested. The campaign went on.

Tolstoy Farm

In prison, Gandhi read two more books which deepened and reinforced his convictions: Henry Thoreau's *Civil Disobedience* and Leo Tolstoy's *The Kingdom of God Is Within You*. He started writing to Tolstoy, a successful Russian author who had given away his possessions, given up tobacco, alcohol and meat, and adopted a simpler life on a farm.

When Gandhi was released he used money from a German friend to set up another commune, this time in the Transvaal, which he called Tolstoy Farm. It was intended partly as a refuge for released and penniless *satyagrahis*, partly as another experiment in living. The residents built their own homes, grew their own food and made their own clothes. Gandhi baked bread, made marmalade and taught the children. He began to **fast** regularly during this period, believing that this cleared his mind and purified his soul. His diet was now restricted to fruit, nuts, olive oil and cereal.

◀ *Gandhi's wife Kasturbai and their four sons – left to right, Harilal, Ramdas, Devadas and Manilal – in South Africa, 1902.*

Victory in South Africa

The registration issue simmered for several years, before being submerged in a wider dispute. First, it was announced that former indentured labourers (see box on page 16) would have to continue paying a high tax simply to stay in South Africa. Secondly, new measures were introduced to restrict Indian movement between the provinces. Finally, in 1913, the highest court in South Africa refused to recognize non-Christian marriages, such as Indian marriages, which were not registered with the government. The Indian community was outraged, and Gandhi launched a new satyagraha campaign.

It lasted over a year, and ended in at least a partial victory. The arrest and imprisonment in concentration camps of thousands of Indians alarmed politicians in London, and pressure was put on the South African administration to compromise. This seemed to put the Indians in a strong position, but when a strike by white South African miners further weakened the government's position, Gandhi called off the campaign. It was not right, he said, to profit from others' troubles. Smuts and the other South African leaders were so impressed by this that they agreed to give in on the tax and marriage issues.

In July 1914, Gandhi finally left South Africa for the last time. 'The saint has left our shores,' Smuts said. 'I hope for ever,' he added.

◀ South Africa's minister in charge of Indian affairs, Jan Christian Smuts, who considered Gandhi a worthy opponent.

A more than worthy opponent

'It was my fate to be the antagonist [opponent] of a man for whom even then I had the highest respect ... He never forgot the human background of the situation, never lost his temper or succumbed to hate, and preserved his gentle humour even in the most trying situations. His manner and spirit ... contrasted markedly with the ruthless and brutal forcefulness which is the vogue in our day ...'

(General Jan Smuts, writing in the 1930s)

6 Homecoming

Gandhi arrived in England two days after World War I broke out, but his offer to form another Indian ambulance corps was refused. In December, he and his family set sail for India, and during the long voyage he must have thought a great deal about his country and his own role in influencing its future.

Several years earlier he had written a pamphlet called *Hind Swaraj* or *Indian Home Rule*, in which he had argued for a semi-independent India within the **Empire**. Although this seemed progressive, some of his other recommendations – a return to small-scale **cottage industry**, the abolition of the railways, and the maintenance of **caste** – were less so. How would he be received in his own country? On arrival, he visited the old **nationalist** leader Gokhale, whom he had already met on several occasions. Gokhale told Gandhi to take a good long look at India, and to keep his ears open and his mouth shut for a whole year.

Sabarmati

Gandhi took the advice. For a year he criss-crossed India, talking and listening to people, always travelling third class. He no longer wore European clothes, just a simple *dhoti* and cap. He spoke English only when it was absolutely necessary.

India in the early 20th century

The growth of administration and business in the late 19th and early 20th centuries had seen the creation of a small and often English-educated Indian middle class, but the vast majority of Indians still lived in villages lacking the most basic facilities, like running water, electricity, or a road to the outside world. Since the early 19th century there had been British promises of greater responsibility for Indians, but in 1915 they still held only 5% of the posts in the Indian Civil Service.

YOU CAN LOCATE THE PLACES WHERE GANDHI WENT IN INDIA ON THE MAP ON PAGE 40.

The India he found did not impress him. So many things were neglected and filthy – railway compartments, **temples**, even the sacred Ganges River at Benares. The **Untouchables** were still living off others' rubbish.

As in South Africa, he decided to lead by example, establishing an *ashram* (**spiritual** community) at Sabarmati in his native Gujarat. The residents agreed to live by the same principles of **self-sufficiency**, **celibacy** and non-violence, to renounce meat and alcohol, and to stress cleanliness. They also **vowed** to reject 'untouchability', but when Gandhi admitted a family of Untouchables some people left the *ashram* in protest and its financial sponsors withdrew their support. Gandhi was still wondering how the community was going to survive when a rich and sympathetic **Muslim** drove up in his car one day, opened the window and handed over a bundle of banknotes.

His own room at the *ashram* was no larger than a cell, with a small terrace outside, on which he slept and worked. His relationship with Kasturbai had slowly grown closer over the years. She still sometimes resented his high-handedness, but was more inclined to listen to his ideas, particularly now that so many other people looked up to him.

▶ *Gandhi and his wife Kasturbai on their return to India in early 1915.*

Gandhi was less successful as a father, particularly with elder sons Harilal and Manilal. He expected them to behave like independent adults, but refused to let them make their own decisions, particularly where marriage partners were concerned. Harilal ended up an alcoholic who did his best to shame his father; Manilal was sent back to South Africa for most of the next 25 years to edit *Indian Opinion*. Devadas and Ramdas were only teenagers at this time, and would benefit from Gandhi becoming more tolerant as he grew older.

Speaking out

In early 1916, Gandhi was invited to speak at the opening of the Hindu University in Benares, and he used the occasion to express his anger. India was enslaved, poor, dirty and uneducated, he said. There would be no real hope for the country until his well-dressed audience stripped themselves of their jewellery. His speech was interrupted by angry shouts. Many walked out in protest.

▲ *The holy city of Benares (now Varanasi) where Gandhi addressed the Hindu University on 6 February 1916.*

He took much the same message to the annual meeting of the **Indian National Congress** in Lucknow. It would be the farmers that would save India, Gandhi said, not the lawyers and doctors and other professionals who had previously made up the nationalist movement.

Without the farmers, independence would just be a matter of handing power from the British middle class to the Indian middle class, and India would follow Britain down the western road of **industrialism** and **materialism**. A real independence would involve more than that. It would involve India following her own, more spiritual path.

Champaran

In 1915, the famous Indian poet Tagore had publicly called Gandhi a *mahatma*, or 'great soul', and by the end of 1916 his growing reputation as a defender of the poor encouraged many to ask for his help. One **peasant** was particularly persistent, following Gandhi around until he agreed to visit the Champaran district, where **indigo** farmers were in dispute with their English landlords. Gandhi quickly discovered that the landlords were indeed demanding excessive rents, and that the lawyers the peasants had hired to help them were just as corrupt.

◀ *The Indian writer and philosopher Rabindranath Tagore, who gave Gandhi the name 'Mahatma', meaning 'great soul'.*

Gandhi was arrested by the local administration, but the **Viceroy** in Delhi, fearing wider trouble, ordered his release. Gandhi then went on to hear some 7000 complaints, and to put together a convincing case on their behalf. The landlords were forced to admit they had been in the wrong, and to pay back at least some of the excessive rents they had charged.

No reward

World War I was now nearing its end, and Gandhi hoped that when peace came Indian loyalty would be repaid by a measure of **home rule**. He was disappointed. In 1918, the world economy was in bad shape, a flu epidemic was killing millions, and revolution seemed to be spreading around the globe. The British, far from introducing home rule, took a harder line with Indian nationalism. Gandhi knew the nationalists had to respond, but how?

Saying no

*'What I did was a very ordinary thing.
I declared that the British could not order
me about in my own country.'*
(Gandhi, on his actions in Champaran)

7 Non-cooperation

On 18 March 1919, the Rowlatt Bills became law. They introduced, among other things, trial without jury. That night, the idea of a nationwide *hartal*, or general strike, came to Gandhi in a dream. On the chosen day, no one would go to work and no shops would open. India would grind to a halt for one day, and after that a *satyagraha* campaign would unfold according to circumstances.

YOU CAN LOCATE THE SITES OF GANDHI'S CAMPAIGNS ON THE MAP ON PAGE 40.

The *hartal* was fixed for 30 March, then changed to 6 April, but in Delhi it went ahead on the original date. Government troops fired on one peaceful demonstration, killing nine people, and in the days that followed there were violent riots. The nationwide event on 6 April, though peaceful in most places, also led to violent disturbances in the Punjab, and when Gandhi was prevented from reaching Delhi by the British, the trouble spread still further. Trains were blocked, shops looted and government offices burnt down.

The Indian people, Gandhi decided, were not ready for the self-discipline of a *satyagraha* campaign. He had made a 'Himalayan miscalculation'.

The Amritsar Massacre

If so, he was not the only one. In the Punjabi city of Amritsar the *hartal* passed peacefully, but over the next few days two Punjabi leaders were deported from the province, a protesting crowd was fired on, and three Englishmen were murdered. On 13 April, a peaceful mass meeting in an enclosed square, the Jallianwalla Bagh, was attacked by troops under the command of General Dyer. He was trying to teach the Indians a lesson, he reported to his superior: 379 were killed and 1137 wounded.

▲ *This still from the film* Gandhi *shows British troops firing on unarmed demonstrators at Amritsar.*

Mass murder

Hunter Commission: *'From time to time you changed your firing and directed it to the place where the crowd was thickest?'*

General Dyer: *'That is so.'*

Hunter Commission:: *'Suppose the passage [the entrance to the square] was sufficient to allow the armoured cars to go in, would you have opened fire with the machine guns?'*

General Dyer: *'I think, probably, yes.'*

(General Dyer replying to questions from members of the Hunter Commission, which was set up by the British government to investigate the Amritsar Massacre)

The lesson Indians learnt was the opposite of that intended. 'When a government takes up arms against its unarmed subjects then it has forfeited the right to govern,' Gandhi said, and few if any Indians disagreed with him. The British still had the power to rule India, but any lingering belief in their right to rule died in the dust of the Jallianwalla Bagh.

Two struggles

Gandhi's next move, in November 1919, was to announce a policy of **non-cooperation** with British rule. Indian law cases were decided outside British courts, and Indian soldiers refused to serve in the British Army. Indians stopped buying British goods, which badly effected some industries in Britain. Gandhi sent back the medal he had won in the **Boer War** and organized a National Volunteer Corps to spread the word throughout the country.

▲ *People in Delhi in the early 1920s, demonstrating their support for Gandhi.*

Enormous amounts of imported British cloth were burnt on ceremonial bonfires. If Indians spun their own cloth, Gandhi said, they could both defy the British and assert their own independence in a peaceful and positive way. The spinning wheel or *charkha* became the symbol of Indian **nationalism** at that time.

Gandhi took a closer interest in **Congress**, which he decided should serve as a nationwide school for teaching the principles of *satyagraha*. In 1920, he rewrote the party's constitution, making it possible for anyone to join by paying a small token sum. Now the poor majority of India's population could contribute to the two parallel struggles Gandhi believed Indians were engaged in – the eviction of the British and the renewal of India.

Chauri Chaura

The campaign of non-cooperation continued through 1920 and 1921, with increasing disruption. Although thousands were arrested, including Gandhi, the campaign went on. When the Prince of Wales visited India in 1921, he paraded through empty streets.

The British treatment of their opponents grew increasingly brutal: the number of beatings and floggings rose sharply, both inside and outside the overflowing prisons. But there was no sign that the British contemplated surrender, and Congress decided to move from non-cooperation to outright **civil disobedience**. The original plan was to mount the campaign throughout India, but Gandhi persuaded the other leaders to restrict it to one area, Bardoli.

The campaign had barely started when news arrived of an atrocity 1280 kilometres (800 miles) away in the small town of Chauri Chaura. A group of Indian policemen who had fired on a demonstration had then been hacked to pieces by a Nationalist mob.

A shocked Gandhi called off all active resistance to the British. The events at Chauri Chaura, he said, showed 'the way India may easily go, if drastic precautions are not taken'. The Indian people were still not ready for true independence.

▶ *Gandhi and his wife Kasturbai in 1922.*

Gandhi's abandonment of the campaign was not popular with many of his supporters, and the British took the opportunity to arrest and try him for **sedition**. '**Non-cooperation** with evil is much a duty as is cooperation with good', he told the court, but he made no attempt to deny his guilt. On the contrary, he asked for the severest possible punishment. The judge reluctantly sentenced him to six years, adding that if the government decided to reduce the term 'no one would be better pleased than I'.

In the event Gandhi served less than two years in Yeravda Prison, and he enjoyed them a great deal. After years of exhausting travel and all the stresses and strains of leadership, it was a welcome rest. Unlike most Indian prisoners, Gandhi was treated well in prison. He had time to meditate, to read and write, to pray and spin; the only punishment was the loss of freedom.

In January 1924, however, he developed appendicitis, and underwent an operation. His recovery was slow and the British, fearing he might die in their custody, hurried to release him.

◀ *Gandhi at his spinning wheel. He encouraged his people to make their own cloth rather than use expensive British imported cloth.*

Hindus and Muslims

Recuperating near Bombay, Gandhi learnt from other **Congress** leaders what had been happening during his imprisonment. The non-cooperation movement had, for the moment, died. More seriously for the long term, the cooperation between **Hindus** and **Muslims**, widespread in 1918–19, had been replaced by growing mistrust. Violent **inter-communal** riots were becoming more frequent.

Gandhi believed that independence was unthinkable with the Hindus and Muslims in conflict, and he took dramatic action to heal the split, announcing he would undertake a 21-day **fast** for Hindu–Muslim friendship. He was now 55 years old, and had not yet fully recovered from his operation. As the fast unfolded, the nation held its breath and enormous pressure was put on both Hindu and Muslim leaders to publicly swallow their differences. One by one they pledged to live in brotherhood.

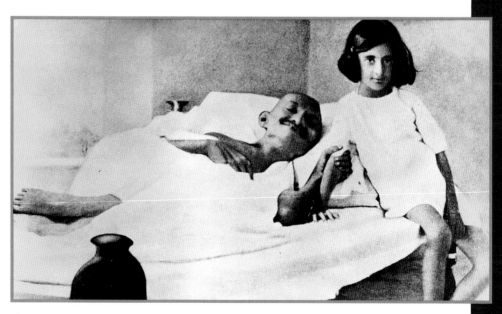

▲ Gandhi recovering from a fast in 1924 in the company of Nehru's 6-year-old daughter Indira. She eventually married another, unrelated, Gandhi, and became Prime Minister of India as Indira Gandhi.

A political guru

Gandhi made no attempt to revive non-cooperation; the time, he realized, was not right. He concentrated instead on preparing his country for the future. He resigned from the political leadership of Congress and for the next five years divided his time between travel around India and the *ashram* at Sabarmati. Kasturbai usually stayed at the *ashram*, but Ramdas and Devadas often accompanied their father on his travels.

On his journeys through the villages Gandhi argued for Hindu–Muslim unity, spoke against 'untouchability' (staying in the homes of **Untouchables** whenever he could) and encouraged everyone to spin cotton each day. He preached the virtues of **self-sufficiency** and hygiene, and discouraged the use of alcohol and drugs. He promoted both the equality of women and the use of **Hindustani** as a national alternative to English. He also supplied useful amateur medical advice. In the rare moments he had to himself he would read and write letters.

At the *ashram* life was simpler and less tiring. Gandhi was the natural leader, but he peeled potatoes and did his chores like everyone else. He was strict about punctuality, cleanliness, not wasting money and spinning daily, but when it came to ideas and beliefs he was almost incredibly tolerant. There were many long-term visitors to the *ashram* who shared neither his faith in God, nor his love of Muslims, nor his belief in non-violence. He would argue good-naturedly with them all.

Gandhi's quick wit was legendary. When a doctor told him that if all sick people simply went to bed they would get better, he replied: 'Don't say that out loud – you'll lose all your patients.'

A year's warning

Early in 1928, a commission headed by Sir John Simon was sent from Britain to study conditions in British India and make recommendations for political reform. The British expected the Indians to be pleased, but they were enraged by the fact that the Simon Commission contained not a single Indian. An almost unanimous decision was made by **Nationalists** not to cooperate with it in any way, and in February 1928 Gandhi announced the beginning of a new *satyagraha* campaign against British tax increases in the Bardoli region.

The year 1928 was a tumultuous one in India. As the new campaign gathered momentum, the travels of the Simon Commission sparked protests and riots. Many were arrested. The government was forced to climb down in Bardoli, but Gandhi, perhaps remembering the violence of earlier years, was reluctant to mount a nationwide campaign. He agreed with the other Congress leaders to give the British a year's warning. If they had not granted India **dominion status** by the end of 1929, then he would lead a non-violent war against them.

March to the sea

In October 1929, with the deadline fast approaching, the **Viceroy** Lord Irwin announced that India would eventually be given dominion status. It was too little, too late. On 1 January 1930, Jawaharlal Nehru, the newly elected President of Congress, proclaimed India's declaration of independence, and the country waited for Gandhi to make the first move in a new campaign of **civil disobedience**.

Two months later, on 12 March, he set off from Sabarmati with 70 members of the *ashram* and walked south towards the sea to gather salt. Both the viceroy and other Congress leaders had laughed when they heard of his plan, but it proved the most effective of all Gandhi's *satyagraha* demonstrations.

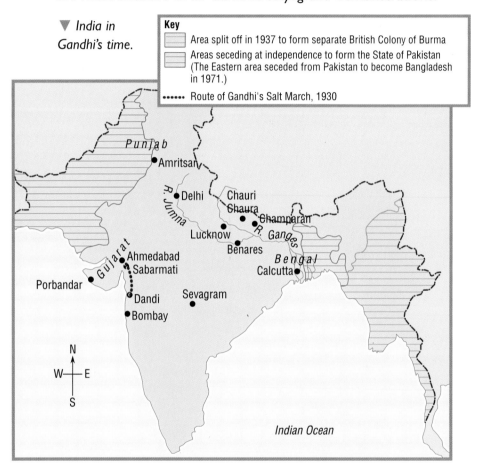

▼ *India in Gandhi's time.*

Key

⬜ Area split off in 1937 to form separate British Colony of Burma

⬜ Areas seceding at independence to form the State of Pakistan (The Eastern area seceded from Pakistan to become Bangladesh in 1971.)

•••••• Route of Gandhi's Salt March, 1930

Punjab
• Amritsar
R. Jumna • Delhi — Chauri Chaura
Lucknow • Champaran
R. Ganges
Benares
Gujarat • Ahmedabad
▲ Sabarmati
Bengal
Calcutta •
Porbandar •
Dandi
Sevagram •
• Bombay

N
W — E
S

Indian Ocean

All Indians understood the importance of salt for both humans and animals in a hot climate, and the British control and tax of salt seemed as unreasonable as a tax on air or water would have been. By the time Gandhi and his followers reached the coast at Dandi a month later, the whole nation was watching. In the weeks after he picked up his illegal handful from the beach, a hundred thousand Indians –

including his sons Manilal, Ramdas and Devadas – went to prison for following his example. The infamous mass beating at the Dharasana saltworks only drove the lesson home. British rule was unjust, unnecessary and unwanted.

The British hosted a **round table conference** on the future of India later that year, but with all the Congress leaders in prison there was no chance of any meaningful progress. The authorities in London reluctantly informed the viceroy that he would have to do a deal with Gandhi.

▲ *Gandhi breaks the tax laws by picking up a handful of natural salt at Dandi, on the west coast of India.*

Dharasana

'In complete silence, the Gandhi men drew up and halted a hundred yards from the stockade. A picked column advanced from the crowd, waded the ditches, and approached the barbed wire stockade .... *Suddenly, at a word of command, scores of native policemen rushed upon the advancing marchers and rained blows on their heads with their steelshod* **lathis**. *Not one of the marchers even raised an arm to fend off the blows. They went down like ninepins. From where I stood I heard the thickening whack of the clubs on unprotected skulls.'*

(Journalist Webb Miller, observing *satyagraha* in action at the Dharasana Saltworks, where two demonstrators were killed and hundreds wounded on 21 May 1930)

Early in 1931, Gandhi and Lord Irwin met eight times. The agreement they reached was called the Delhi Pact: in return for Gandhi calling off the *satyagraha* campaign, Irwin promised to release all prisoners, return confiscated property and allow the collection of salt from India's beaches. There was no mention of independence, but that would be discussed by a second **round table conference** later in the year.

Fall from grace

'[England] is no longer regarded as the champion throughout the world of fair dealing and the exponent of high principle, but as the upholder of Western race supremacy and the exploiter of those outside her own borders.'

(Indian poet Rabindranath Tagore, speaking to the *Manchester Guardian* in May 1930)

Many British people welcomed this apparent softening of their Government's attitude, but one prominent political figure did not. Winston Churchill, commenting on Gandhi's meetings with Irwin, spoke of 'the nauseating and humiliating spectacle of this one-time Inner Temple lawyer, now **seditious fakir**, striding half-naked up the steps of the **Viceroy's** palace, there to negotiate and to parley on equal terms with the representative of the **King-Emperor**.'

Nor were Gandhi's enemies all British. Many members of India's minority communities, particularly the **Muslims** and **Untouchables**, thought the **Hindus** might prove worse rulers than the British, and leaders of these communities were determined to safeguard their rights before independence was granted. Before leaving for London, Gandhi reluctantly accepted a **separate electorate** for Muslims. Only this, the Muslims thought, would ensure their voices were heard in the government of an independent India.

England

Accompanied by his son Devadas, Gandhi left for London at the end of August and stayed in England for 84 days. On a personal level his visit was a huge success. His hosts had provided him with a lavish suite at the Ritz Hotel, but he chose instead to stay at a community centre in London's poverty-stricken East End. He strode out every morning in his **loincloth**, ahead of his exhausted police escort, and talked to everyone he met. The children called him Uncle Gandhi and asked him where his trousers were.

During his time in England Gandhi met several famous people, including the film comedian Charlie Chaplin and ex-Prime Minister Lloyd George, and was invited to Buckingham Palace for tea with the King and Queen. When a reporter asked Gandhi if he had worn enough clothes for the occasion, he replied that the King had been wearing enough for both of them!

▼ *Gandhi surrounded by new friends in London's East End.*

He addressed several meetings, spent two weekends at Oxford arguing with professors, and visited a Lancashire textile mill that had been badly affected by the Indian boycotts of British cloth. At the end of one meeting, a worker announced: 'I am one of the unemployed, but if I was in India I would say the same thing that Mr Gandhi is saying.' Everywhere Gandhi went, people admired him.

Deadlock

The round table conference was much less successful. The British Government was reluctant to make any definite promises about reform, and various other Indian groups now shared the Muslim desire for separate electorates. Gandhi hated this idea: he wanted Indians to rise above their divisions, not give in to them. When the conference ended without agreement, he called it 'the most humiliating day of my life'.

▼ *Gandhi at the round table conference, September 1931. This was one of his 'silent Mondays' and the man sitting on his left, Pandit Malaviya, was his spokesman for the day.*

Back in India, Gandhi was arrested without charge or trial. Lord Willingdon, Irwin's less knowledgeable successor as viceroy, was determined there should be no new campaign following the failure of the conference. **Congress** was outlawed and soon 35,000 of its members were behind bars.

In prison, Gandhi worried about the divisions among Indians. He was particularly concerned about the **Untouchables**, who now had their own organization led by Bhimrao Ambedkar. When the British agreed to separate electorates in provincial elections for the Untouchables, Gandhi was appalled. He understood the Untouchables' concern – few Indians were as ready to accept them as he was – but he was convinced **segregation** was not the answer. On 20 September 1932, he announced that he would **fast unto death** against the decision.

Children of God

Gandhi lay on a white iron cot under the shade of a mango tree in the Yeravda Prison yard. He was 63 years old now, and by the fourth day of the fast his doctors were seriously worried. All India held its breath as various political leaders desperately sought the compromise that would save him. On the sixth day they found it: the separate electorates would be a purely temporary measure. On the seventh day, Gandhi allowed Kasturbai to bring him a glass of orange juice.

The political deal was only a small part of the story. Gandhi's fast had inspired people all over India to open their **temples** to those they called Untouchables, and whom he called *harijans* or 'children of God'. Prominent people accepted food from *harijan* hands, hundreds of villages decided to let *harijans* use their wells. The 'scourge of Hinduism', as Gandhi called it, had received a serious blow.

Gandhi was released from prison in May 1933. His critics could claim that after four years of protest and negotiation India had still achieved neither independence nor the promise of it. But independence was nearer, and so, in Gandhi's mind, was a better India. He had no use of one without the other.

On the road

While Gandhi was in prison, the British had decided to tax the thriving Sabarmati *ashram*. When the residents refused to pay, their assets were seized. After his release Gandhi ordered the abandonment of the *ashram*, telling his followers to spread themselves across the villages of India.

In 1934, he resigned his seat in Congress, confident that his friend Jawaharlal Nehru could handle the political side of things while he concentrated on reforming India. For most of the next six years he crossed India on foot, rather like a wandering *sadhu* (holy man). In village after village he promoted small-scale industry and repeated his familiar messages of religious tolerance and love. In 1936, he established a new *ashram* at Sevagram in central India. Kasturbei and Gandhi, very close partners during this period, came to consider Sevagram home.

Pakistan

In the political world there was some progress towards independence: the 1935 India Act offered the Indians a measure of self-rule but real power remained with the British. Gandhi commented that India was still a prison, but that the inmates were now allowed to elect their jailers. Despite this, Congress agreed to contest the new elections, and won majorities in nine of India's eleven provinces.

▲ *Gandhi (right) with the Indian politician Jawaharlal Nehru. The two men disagreed on many things, but they loved and trusted each other.*

Significantly, the **Muslim League** won only 5 per cent of the Muslim vote. Its leader, Mohammed Jinnah, desperate to remain in power, fuelled Muslim fears of Hindu rule, and focused those fears into calls for an independent Muslim state of Pakistan. The scene was set for the final round of India's fight for independence.

Two Gandhian thoughts

'*Caste has nothing to do with religion in general and Hinduism in particular. It is a sin to believe anyone else is inferior or superior to ourselves.*'

'*Religions are different roads converging to the same point. What does it matter that we take different roads as long as we reach the same goal. In reality, there are as many different religions as there are individuals.*'

A light in the darkness

When World War II broke out in September 1939, the British **viceroy** in Delhi declared that India, like Britain, was now at war with Germany. Gandhi's belief in non-violence was now stronger than any sense of loyalty he felt to Britain, and he opposed any Indian participation in the war. However, most of the other **Congress** leaders were prepared to support Britain in exchange for a promise of independence when the war ended.

The British, however, failed to make such a promise, and majority Indian opinion slowly turned against them. By 1942, Congress was united behind Gandhi's 'Quit India' campaign of **civil disobedience**. When Gandhi was arrested, the country erupted in a series of violent protests.

Family ties

Kasturbai addressed a meeting in her husband's place, and was imprisoned in Yeravda, alongside Gandhi. In February 1944, she died in his arms, of acute bronchitis. The early years of their long marriage had been punctuated with disagreements and periods apart, but in later life they shared beliefs and were inseparable.

As a father Gandhi had also improved with age. There was no hope of reconciliation with his alcoholic eldest son Harilal, but second son Manilal found Gandhi a much more loving father when he returned from South Africa in 1945. Younger sons Ramdas and Devadas had been better favoured. One or both had been at their father's side throughout the great campaigns of the 1920s and early 1930s.

Independence and tragedy

Gandhi, still grieving, was released from prison in May 1944. Fifteen months later the war was over, and in Britain a new Labour Government was eager to speed up India's transition to independence. However, Jinnah's **Muslim League** was now determined on **partition** – the division of India into **Hindu** and **Muslim** countries. When the British, supported by Gandhi, Nehru and Congress, disagreed with partition, the Muslim League called for direct action, and Hindu–Muslim clashes increased in both number and violence, particularly in the finely balanced provinces of Bengal and the Punjab.

▲ *Gandhi with Muslim leader Muhammad Jinnah, whom he failed to persuade against partition.*

Gandhi toured Bengal, promoting peace and sanity, but through 1946 and 1947 the violence escalated. Faced with the alternative of **civil war**, Congress reluctantly accepted partition. Gandhi refused to join the Independence Day celebrations in Delhi, calling the day 'a **spiritual** tragedy'.

▲ *Bodies littering Chitpore Road in Calcutta, after Hindu–Muslim riots in August 1946 had resulted in over 3000 deaths.*

YOU CAN LOCATE THE PLACES WHERE GANDHI WENT IN INDIA ON THE MAP ON PAGE 40.

Gandhi had come to Calcutta – a Hindu city with a large Muslim minority – fearing there would be trouble. At first his presence had a calming effect, but the violence raging across large areas of India reached the city, and Gandhi decided only a **fast unto death** could bring the people back to their senses. He ended his **fast** only when the Hindu and Muslim leaders promised in writing to live in peace with each other.

Gandhi travelled west, hoping to perform a similar miracle in the riot-torn Punjab, but the death and destruction in Delhi forced him to break his journey. In January 1948, he once again fasted unto death, and once again the various leaders sat by his bed and promised to respect the lives and property of other communities. By this time the country was mostly at peace, but the cost had been enormous – at least a million people had died in the violent clashes of 1947.

Death

In Delhi, Gandhi had concentrated on saving the Muslim minority from the Hindu majority, and some Hindus thought he had betrayed them. Two days after he broke his fast, a Hindu extremist was arrested for trying to throw a bomb into the daily prayer meeting. 'If I fall victim to an assassin's bullet,' Gandhi said afterwards, 'there must be no anger within me. God must be in my heart and on my lips.'

At a prayer meeting ten days later, another Hindu extremist stepped forward and shot him three times in the stomach and heart. Gandhi collapsed, murmured the words 'Oh God', and died.

His body was burnt in a traditional ceremony by the River Jumna, and most of his ashes scattered at the meeting of the Jumna and Ganges rivers. Some ashes were given to family and friends, but requests for ashes from around the world had to be refused. In death, as in life, there was not enough of Gandhi to go around.

◄ Gandhi with two young relatives just one day before his death.

No ordinary light

'The light has gone out of our lives and there is darkness everywhere and I do not quite know what to tell you and how to say it. Our beloved leader, Bapu [father] as we call him, is no more ... The light has gone out, I said, and yet I was wrong. For the light that shone in this country was no ordinary light.'

(Jawaharlal Nehru, addressing India on the radio on the evening of Gandhi's death, 30 January 1948)

Gandhi played a crucial role in winning independence from the British. From the time of his return to India in 1915, through the great **non-cooperation** campaigns of the 1920s and 1930s, he not only made it difficult for the British to rule India, he also made them doubt their right to do so. Using original and highly creative tactics, he seized the moral high ground and also made a mockery of British pretensions to a higher civilization.

He also pushed his own countrymen to change. Time and again he forced the **Hindus** and **Muslims** to be aware of each others' rights, and he could hardly be blamed for the fact that their mutual distrust proved stronger. In a similar way, he forced his fellow Hindus to face the reality of their centuries-long mistreatment of the **Untouchables**, and for this alone he deserved an honoured place in history.

▲ A statue of Gandhi in the Indian city of Bangalore, showing him marching on one of his campaigns.

Gandhi's use of mass campaigns, which necessarily involved the participation of Indians at all levels of society, paved the way for democracy in the post-independence years. But in most other respects independent India is far from what he hoped it would be. Shortly before his death he talked of 'the vain imitation of the tinsel of the West', and under Nehru and successive leaders India has indeed pursued economic development on the Western model. Central government control has grown stronger, and there has been little development of small-scale industry in the villages. The **caste** system still affects Indian society, women remain far from equal, and **inter-communal** violence continues to erupt from time to time with frightening intensity.

A hard act to follow

In later life, Gandhi had a worldwide reputation, and his inspiration has helped others since his death. Martin Luther King Jr., the American civil rights leader, ran his own campaigns against **race discrimination** as Gandhi did, using 'the force of truth' as his only weapon. He too set his people free; tragically, he too was gunned down by the forces of prejudice and ignorance.

Role model

'Gandhi was inevitable. If humanity is to progress, Gandhi is inescapable. He lived, thought and acted, inspired by a vision of humanity evolving towards a world of peace and harmony. We may ignore him at our risk.'

(Martin Luther King Jr.)

In the latter half of the 20th century, Gandhi's principles were more often conspicuous by their absence. Most of the many independence struggles which took place used armed force, and when Gandhi's tactics have been used – as, for example, in the Irish Republican Army **fasts unto death** of the 1980s – they were part of a wider campaign of violence. No major new 'Gandhi' has risen to prominence in any of the world's long-running conflicts, although there have been echoes of his spirit in the work of exiled Tibetan leader the Dalai Lama.

A force for good

Gandhi now seems an old-fashioned figure in some ways; he clearly had his faults and was a man of his time. But the trend towards the increasingly unfeeling, violent and anonymous society of the last half of the 20th century has created its own reaction, and many of the causes which Gandhi fought for – **cottage industry**, peaceful change and a reverence for all life – seem even more widely relevant now than they did in his lifetime. In the West, the increasing interest in small-scale, low-impact economic activity, Eastern religion, **vegetarianism** and animal rights owes at least something to Gandhi's long-term influence. Many individuals throughout the world are still guided by his ideas and principles.

Above all, Gandhi will be remembered for the example he set. He stood for peace against violence, for **spiritual** fulfilment against the empty satisfactions of greed and **materialism**, for truth against the comfort of illusions and the evil of lies. When he thought it necessary to prove a point, he put his own life on the line, not the lives of others. He was a good man who moved the world, an example to all, whether or not they hold positions of power.

▲ The mahatma's room at the ashram in Sevagram, as preserved after his death. His few important possessions – prayer beads, spectacles and boxed spinning wheel – lie on the bed.

Epitaph

'The sudden flash of his death revealed a vast darkness. No one who survived him had tried so hard – and with so much success – to live a life of truth, kindness, self-effacement, humility, service and non-violence throughout a long, difficult struggle against mighty adversaries. He fought passionately and unremittingly against British rule of his country and the evil in his own countrymen. But he kept his own hands clean in the midst of the battle. He fought without malice or falsehood or hate.'

(American journalist Louis Fischer, who met Gandhi on several occasions)

Timeline

1869	Mohandas Kharamchand Gandhi born on 2 October in Porbandar, Gujarat.
1883	Marries Kasturbai Makanji.
1885	Founding of **Indian National Congress**. Gandhi's father dies.
1887	Finishes school and attends Samaldas College for one term.
1888	Birth of first son, Harilal.
1889	Starts studying law in England.
1892	Birth of second son, Manilal.
1893	Takes job in South Africa.
1894	Founds **Natal Indian Congress.**
1896	Brings wife and sons to South Africa.
1897	Birth of third son, Ramdas.
1899	Outbreak of Second **Boer War**. Gandhi forms Indian Ambulance Corps.
1900	Birth of fourth son, Devadas.
1901	Returns to India.
1902	Summoned back to South Africa.
1903	Begins publishing *Indian Opinion*.
1904	Establishes Phoenix Farm.
1907	Launches first *satyagraha* campaign.
1910	Establishes Tolstoy Farm.
1913–14	Second *satyagraha* campaign.
1914	Negotiates Indian Relief Act with Smuts. Outbreak of World War I.
1915	Gandhi returns to India, tours country, establishes *ashram* at Sabarmati.
1916	Speaks at opening of **Hindu** University in Benares.
1917	Campaigns in Champaran on behalf of **indigo** growers.
1918	Rowlatt Bills passed by British Government.

1919	The *hartal* and the Amritsar Massacre.
1920	The **non-cooperation** campaign begins.
1922	The Chauri Chaura incident.
	Gandhi is arrested and imprisoned.
1924	Gandhi **fasts** for Hindu–**Muslim** unity.
	Released from prison.
1925–28	Tours India.
1928	The Simon Commission.
1929	Congress declares Indian independence.
1930	Gandhi opens new campaign with Salt March.
1931	Agrees Delhi Pact; travels to England for round table conference.
1932	Imprisoned.
	Fasts for better treatment of **Untouchables.**
1933–39	Tours India.
1939	Outbreak of World War II.
1942	Gandhi leads 'Quit India' campaign.
	Arrested and imprisoned.
1944	Death of wife Kasturbai.
1945–47	Increasing violence between Hindus and Muslims.
1947	India granted independence.
	Gandhi fasts for communal peace in Calcutta.
1948	Fasts for communal peace in Delhi.
	Gandhi is assassinated on 30 January.

Key people of Gandhi's time

Churchill, Winston Spencer (1874–1965). British politician. During the 1930s Churchill spoke out against the timid policy of successive British governments in both Europe and India. He became prime minister during the crucial early phase of World War II, and opposed any concessions to Indian **nationalism**, famously declaring that he had 'not become the king's first minister in order to preside at the liquidation of the British **Empire**'.

Gokhale, Gopal Krishna (1866–1915). Indian nationalist politician. He was the leader of the moderates in the **Indian National Congress** in the years before World War I. He much admired the young Gandhi, and expected him to eventually become the leader of India's fight for independence.

Jinnah, Muhammad Ali (1876–1948). Indian **Muslim** and Bombay lawyer prominent in the **Muslim League** (founded 1906). In the years following World War I, he was friendly to Congress, but after becoming leader of the League in 1934 his overwhelming priority was the protection of Muslim minority interests after independence. From 1937, he campaigned for a separate Muslim state of Pakistan. The turmoil which followed his Direct Action Day in August 1946 persuaded Congress to accept **partition** and the creation of Pakistan. He became the new state's first governor-general in 1947 but died the following year.

Nehru, Jawaharlal (1889–1964). Indian lawyer and politician. Son of Motilal Nehru, who was also a prominent member of Congress. Like Gandhi, Jawaharlal studied law in England.

Unlike Gandhi, he was an agnostic, a believer in scientific progress and a socialist. Despite these differences there was a strong bond between them. Nehru became involved in the independence struggle in the years following World War I and was imprisoned nine times by the British. He was elected president of Congress in 1929 and announced India's declaration of independence at the end of that year. In 1947 he became Prime Minister of the newly independent India, a post he held until his death in 1964. (Jawaharlal Nehru's daughter Indira Gandhi (no relation to Mohandas) also served as Prime Minister of India (1966–77 and 1980–84.) She was succeeded in the post by her eldest son Rajiv Gandhi (1984–89). Both were assassinated.)

Smuts, Jan (1870–1950). South African soldier and politician. He led **Boer** forces during the second **Boer War** but then became a leading advocate of Anglo-Boer cooperation, a minister in the colonial administration and one of the founders of the Union of South Africa (1909). He served as Prime Minister in the 1930s and played a prominent role in the foundation of both the League of Nations and the United Nations.

Tagore, Rabindranath (1861–1941). Indian writer and philosopher who won the Nobel Prize for Literature in 1913. Knighted in 1915, he returned the honour after the Amritsar Massacre. It was he who named Gandhi the *Mahatma*, the great soul.

Viceroys of India during the struggle for independence

1916–21	Lord Chelmsford	1936–43	Lord Linlithgow
1921–26	Lord Reading	1943–47	Lord Wavell
1926–31	Lord Irwin	1947	Lord Mountbatten
1931–36	Lord Willingdon		

Further reading & other resources

Further reading

Britain 1950–1900 (Living Through History series), Nigel Kelly, Rosemary Rees and Jane Shuter, Heinemann Library, 1998

Martin Luther King Jr. (Leading Lives series), David Downing, Heinemann Library, 2002

Mohandas Gandhi, Catherine Bush, Burke, 1988

Mohandas Gandhi, Glenn Alan Cheney, Franklin Watts, 1982

The Twentieth Century World (Living Through History series), Nigel Kelly, Rosemary Rees and Jane Shuter, Heinemann Library, 1998

Winston Churchill (Leading Lives series), Fiona Reynoldson, Heinemann Library, 2001

Sources

An Autobiography or the Story of My Experiments with Truth, Mohandas Gandhi, Phoenix House, 1949

Gandhi, Father of a Nation, Catherine Clément, Thames and Hudson, 1996

The Life of Mahatma Gandhi, Louis Fischer, HarperCollins, 1997

Websites

Biography and links to pictures:
   www.mkgandhi.org

New York Times article:
   www.nytimes.com/learning/general/specials/india/480131obit
   -gandhi.html

Film

Gandhi (directed by Richard Attenborough, starring Ben Kingsley)

Acknowledgement

The publishers would like to thank Thames and Hudson Ltd for permission to reproduce copyright material on p. 51.

Glossary

amulet piece of jewellery worn as a charm against evil

artisan skilled craftsman

ashram home of a community dedicated to self-improvement through spiritual enlightenment

Bhagavad Gita epic poem considered to be one of Hinduism's most important religious texts

called to the Bar given permission to practise as a lawyer

Boer South African descended from Dutch settlers

(second) Boer War war between Great Britain and the two Boer republics of Transvaal and the Orange Free State (1899–1902)

caste social class in Hindu society. There are four main castes: Brahmins (priests and professionals), Kshatriyas (rulers, warriors and administrators), Vaishyas (farmers and merchants) and Shudras (artisans and labourers).

celibacy not having any sexual relationships

civil disobedience peaceful form of protest usually involving the refusal to obey particular laws or to pay particular taxes

civil war war between different groups within one country

commune community in which living space, possessions and usually ideals are shared

Congress see **Indian National Congress**

cottage industry business carried out within the home

dhoti cloth worn around the hips (loincloth)

dominion status self-government within the British Empire

elocution art of speaking clearly and correctly

(British) Empire several countries ruled by a single king-emperor (and governed by their government) in another country

fakir holy man relying on the charity of others

fast giving up all (or some sorts of) food for a specific period

fast unto death refusing to eat until either specific conditions are met or the person fasting dies

Hindu follower of Hinduism, the main religion and social system of India, which traditionally features multiple gods, a belief in reincarnation and the caste system

Hindustani a particular form of the Hindi language, used as a common language throughout much of India

home rule government of a country by its own citizens

Indian National Congress political organization founded in 1885 to discuss increased Indian participation in the country's government

indigo plant from which blue dye is made

industrialism economic system dominated by manufacturing industries

inter-communal between (usually religious) communities

Islam one of the world's three major monotheistic (one God) religions (along with Christianity and Judaism), founded by the Prophet Mohammed in the 7th century

king-emperor from 1877 to 1947 the British monarch was considered both emperor (or empress) of India and king (or queen) of Britain and its other global possessions

Koran the holy book of Islam

lathi bamboo cane with a steel tip

loincloth cloth worn around the hips

materialism tendency to consider material things (such as possessions and physical comforts) more important than spiritual values

Muslim follower of Islam

Muslim League political organization founded in 1906 to represent the interests of Indian Muslims

Natal Indian Congress political organization founded by Gandhi in 1894 to represent the interests of Indians in Natal

nationalist someone actively working for the advancement of his or her nation, particularly when there is conflict with the interests of foreign ruling power

non-cooperation in India, a refusal to share in the British administration of the country

partition in India, the division of the British-ruled area into India and Pakistan

peasant small farmer or farm worker

petition written request, usually signed by many people

Quakers Society of Friends, a Christian group devoted to peace

racial discrimination treating people badly because they belong to a particular racial group

round table conference assembly for discussion, usually involving all interested parties

satyagraha force of truth (*satya* is truth, *agraha* is force)

satyagrahi fighters whose only weapon is the force of truth

sedition conduct, speech or writing that encourages rebellion

segregation in racial matters, the enforced separation of races

self-sufficiency providing one's own food, clothing and shelter from one's own efforts

separate electorates members of each community voting only in seats which have been set aside for their community, rather than the members of all communities voting in each and every seat

spiritual concerned with the world of the spirit, rather than the world of material things

temple building or place where worship of a god or gods takes place

Untouchables members of the under-class of Indian society, who do the lowliest, dirtiest jobs

vegetarian someone who does not eat meat or fish

viceroy in theory, the king or queen's deputy in India; in practice, the agent of the British Government

vow solemn promise, often to God

Index

Titles in the *Leading Lives* series include:

Hardback   0 431 13865 6

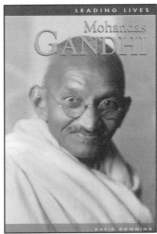

Hardback   0 431 13868 0

Hardback   0 431 13867 2

Hardback   0 431 13864 8

Hardback   0 431 13869 9

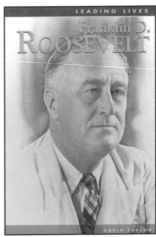

Hardback   0 431 13852 4

Find out about the other titles in this series on our website www.heinemann.co.uk/library